Revealed:
The Passover Seder Haggadah

(A Messianic Jewish Pesach Celebration)

By: Chris Steinmeyer

Copyright © 2019 Chris Steinmeyer

All rights reserved. No part of this publication may be reproduced, stored in a retrieval system, or transmitted in any form or by any means – electronic, mechanical, photocopy, recording, or any other – without prior written permission of the author.

ISBN: 9781660077984

References

AMP - Scripture quotations marked (AMP) are taken from the Amplified Bible, Copyright © 2015 by The Lockman Foundation. Used by permission.

CJB - All Scripture quotations, indicated with (CJB), are taken from the Complete Jewish Bible by David H. Stern. Copyright © 1998. All rights reserved. Used by permission of Messianic Jewish Publishers, 6120 Day Long Lane, Clarksville, MD 21029. www.messianicjewish.net.

NIV - Scripture quotations marked (NIV) are taken from the Holy Bible, New International Version®, NIV®. Copyright © 1973, 1978, 1984, 2011 by Biblica, Inc.™ Used by permission of Zondervan. All rights reserved worldwide, www.zondervan.com. The "NIV" and "New International Version" are trademarks registered in the United States Patent and Trademark Office by Biblica, Inc.™

WEB - World English Bible (WEB). Public domain.

YLT - Young's Literal Translation (YLT). Public domain.

Prayer transliterations and Hebrew compiled by Nathan Steinmeyer and Rozalin Matar Steinmeyer. Used with permission.

Dedication

To my family: Jim, Gabe, Mike, Rose, Nate, and Zack. *Revealed: The Passover Seder Haggadah* was, is, and always will be written at your request. "Mom, you have to write this down." You are <u>all</u> a gift!

Foreword

"Behold, I stand at the door and knock. If anyone hears My voice and opens the door, I will come in and eat with him, and he with Me" (Revelation 3:20, AMP). The call to be a child of God rests upon believers through Yeshua, Jesus the Messiah. Furthermore, the Passover manifests as an essential ingredient to understand the history and prophetic works of God in sanctifying, freeing, redeeming, and adopting His children.

Have you ever asked God what He wanted you to leave behind when you leave earth for heaven? I did. The overwhelming knowledge that I needed to take the Haggadah off the shelf and finish the project settled in my mind. I am not one to predict the future, but what would I leave behind? After all, there are two things guaranteed in life: death and taxes. I choose to leave His story. The story of Adonai and His begotten Son, Yeshua, who intersects time and space to impact a people group. In turn, that people group through highs and lows, mountains and valleys impact the nations.

Yet, the story does not start with where we are today; the story starts in the ancient past. It starts with a God that sanctifies, frees, redeems, and adopts His children from this world into His Kingdom. Nevertheless, it all starts with one person reaching out; one person willing to tell His story.

While my husband studied engineering, Joel and Linda invited our family to join their family for the Jewish Passover Seder. During the Seder meal, something gripped our children's hearts. We returned for the next three years to Joel and Linda's house for the Passover Seder celebration. When we moved, our children wanted to celebrate the Seder in our home with their Dad taking the place that Joel previously occupied.

As time (actually, a decade) progressed, Joel's Haggadah expanded to include historic explanations and connections to the Messiah that exist within the Passover celebration. This expansion helped people understand the importance and significance of Passover. While there are hundreds, if not thousands of Haggadah's due to cultural and linguistic differences, the goal in writing this Haggadah was to combine the historic Jewish celebration with an overlay of history and scripture while drawing the prophetic connection to Jesus the Messiah, *Yeshua HaMashiach*.

The Passover Seder persists as an active celebration. It remains new with every reading. I am consistently amazed at the intricate interweaving of history and prophesy that Adonai creates, and Jesus completes. I remind our children (now adults) that Passover Seder is NOT about great food or a formal dinner. Passover acknowledges the awesome power of Adonai and His ability to sanctify, bless, and redeem His children.

Many people know how to use the Haggadah, but for others the Haggadah constitutes a new adventure. For those unfamiliar with the Haggadah, it is meant to be read aloud. Commonly, the Seder is celebrated around the family table, but it can be used for a couple people to several hundred. Our family Passover Seder generally hosts three to twenty people dependent on the number of friends joining us in our home (once the whole high school football team was invited).

As the Passover Seder correlates to the Jewish calendar, I encourage you to look up the dates of Passover for the current year. While intended for a specific date, sometimes we hold the Passover celebration on different dates so everyone can partake.

I pray that when your family uses *Revealed: The Passover Seder Haggadah* for your Passover liturgy that you are reminded of the absolute power of our Almighty God.

Enjoy!
Chris Steinmeyer

Table of Content

Part 1

Introduction 2

Brechat Haner – Lighting the Candles 5

Urchatz – Washing of the Hands................................ 9

The Invitation 12

Kiddush – The First Cup: The Cup of Sanctification 14

Ma-Nishtanah – The Four Questions 17

Maggid – The Story of Passover............................... 22

Karpas – The Parsley 25

Matzo – The Bread 27

Yachutz – Breaking the Middle Matzo 32

Maror – The Bitter Herb 34

Charoseth 36

The Passover Lamb – The Shank Bone 38

The Ten Plagues 41

The First Plague – Blood, *Dahm* 44

The Second Plague – Frogs, *Tzfardeyah* 46

The Third Plague – Gnats, *Kinim* 48

The Fourth Plague – Beetles, *Arov* 50

The Fifth Plague – Pestilence on Livestock, *Dever* 53

The Sixth Plague – Boils, *Sh'him* 56

The Seventh Plague – Hail, *Barad* 58

The Eighth Plague – Locust, *Arbeh* 60

The Ninth Plague – Darkness, *Hosheh* 63

The Tenth Plague – Slaying of the Firstborn..................... 66

The Second Cup – The Cup of Freedom 70

Part 2

Seulchen Orech – The Meal 77

The Egg 77

Tzaphun – The Afikomen 79

The Third Cup – The Cup of Redemption 84

Part 3

Hillel – Grace after the Meal 90

The Cup of Elijah 93

The Fourth Cup – The Cup of Acceptance 95

Conclusion 97

Appendix

- I – The Questions 101
- II – Glossary 102
- III – Song Lyrics 104
  - *Adir Hu* 104
  - And It Came to Pass at Midnight 109
  - Awesome God 112
  - *Dayenu* 113
  - Days of Elijah 116
  - O Come, O Come Emmanuel 118
  - We Will Glorify the King of King 120
- IV – Instructions 122
- Acknowledgements 130

Part 1

Introduction

Passover is a time for telling stories, traditions, rituals, and celebrations. During Passover, Adonai demonstrated His great power by defeating the gods of Egypt. Passover endures as a time of thanksgiving for Adonai's provisions. Yet, in a broader sense, Passover foreshadows *Yeshua HaMashiach*, Jesus the Messiah, the Passover Lamb that still sanctifies, redeems and delivers His people. Traditionally and scripturally, we "observe the Feast of Unleavened Bread (The Passover), for in this same day I brought your armies out of the land of Egypt. Therefore, you shall observe this day throughout your generations by an ordinance forever" (Exodus 12:17, WEB).

We remember and talk about the Passover of Adonai for Deuteronomy 6:4-7 (WEB) declares, "Hear, Oh Israel; Adonai is our God …. love Adonai with all your heart, and with all your soul, and with all your strength. These words, which I command you today shall be on your hearts; and you shall teach them diligently to your children, and talk of them when you sit in your house, and when you walk by the way and when you lie down, and when you rise up." In obedience to the commandment of Deuteronomy 6:4-9, let us begin the Passover Seder by stating the declaration of faith in the One and Only God.

Hear O Israel, Adonai is our God, Adonai alone. Blessed be the Name of His glorious majesty forever and ever.

Shma Yisrail, Adonai Eloheinu, Adonai echad. barukh shem kvod malkhuto lolam vaed.

שמע ישראל יהיה אלוהינו, יהיה אחד. ברוך שם כבוד מלכותו לעולם ועד

The Feast of Unleavened Bread (The Passover) is a weeklong celebration. The Passover Seder, the meal within the Passover celebration, provides the climax and the continuity between the present, the past, and the dramatic, miraculous events that led to the exodus of the children of Israel from Egypt over 4000 years ago. With this event, the God of Abraham, Isaac, and Jacob changed the lives of His people forever. Adonai sealed the Israelites with the blood of the Passover lamb, thus, saving them from the curse that befell pharaoh.

The original Passover lamb remains a symbolic portrayal of the ultimate Passover Lamb, Yeshua, who redeemed and delivered His people from the slavery of sin and eternal death. Adonai rescued the Israelites from physical slavery in Egypt. Today, Yeshua rescues us from the enslavement of self, culture and sin. Yeshua commands us to "proclaim the good news to all creation" (Mark 16:15, YLT) and build the kingdom of God. Therefore, we remember and celebrate the Passover Seder each year.

The Passover Seder
Brechat Haner – Lighting the Candles

We welcome the Passover by lighting special holiday candles. The candles commemorate the light we received from Adonai. This light represents the command to be the light of the world. The Old Testament prophet Isaiah challenged the Hebrew people with Adonai's command to bring the light of the world - the gift of salvation - to all people even the Gentiles. Isaiah 49:6 (AMP) declares, "I will also make you a light to the nations that My salvation may reach to the ends of the earth." Yeshua extended this command when He reaffirmed in Matthew 5:14 (WEB) that "You are the light of the world. A city on a hill can't be hidden." Therefore, we light the candles, a light that cannot be hidden, to represent the light of Adonai for the whole world.

Traditionally, the woman of the house lights the candles because the first messianic prophesy in the Garden of Eden foreshadowed Adonai's salvation for the woman and her offspring when Adonai addressed the serpent (Satan) in Genesis 3:15 (WEB), "I will put hostility between you and the woman, and between your offspring and her offspring. He will bruise your head, and you will bruise his heel." Furthermore, Isaiah 7:14 (WEB) acknowledges that "the virgin will conceive and bear a son and shall call his name Immanuel" which means God with us. Matthew 1:22-23 confirms that history and prophecy meet with the birth of Yeshua, Jesus of Nazareth.

The woman of the house recites this prayer. If the Passover falls on a Friday evening (Sabbath), then the words in parentheses are included.

Blessed are You, Adonai our God, King of the universe, who sanctified us by Your commandments and commands us to be a light to the nations and gave to us *Yeshua HaMashiach*, Jesus the Messiah, the light of the world. Therefore, I light the (Sabbath and) festive candles. Amen!

Baruch atah Adonai Eloheinu melech haolam, asher kidshanu al yadei amunah ba-Yeshua hamashiach, or ha-olam, oubashmo anu madliqim ner shel pesach.

ברוך אתה אדוני מלך העולם, אשר קידשנו על ידי אמונה בישוע המשיח, אור העולם, ובשמו אנו מדליקים נר של פסח.

Optional song: Psalm 24:1-6 (WEB)

> The earth is Adonai's, with its fullness;
>> the world, and those who dwell in it.
>> For he has founded it on the seas,
>> and established it on the floods.
>
> Who may ascend to Adonai's hill?
>> Who may stand in his holy place?
>> He who has clean hands and a pure heart;
>> who has not lifted up his soul to falsehood,
>> and has not sworn deceitfully.
>> He shall receive a blessing from Adonai,
>> righteousness from the God of his salvation.

This is the generation of those who seek Him, who seek your face.

חי

Urchatz – **Washing of the Hands**

(The woman of the house brings a pitcher of water, a basin, and a towel)

At the entrance to the Temple in Jerusalem there stood a great basin in which the priests washed their hands before entering the Holy of Holies. Likewise, the head of the house washes his hands. The father of the house is the priest of the house presenting his family before Adonai. While this seems like a simple act, washing the hands bears a profound significance in both the Old and the New Testaments. The ceremonial washing of the hands resides within the process for the atonement of unjust murder and the shedding of innocent blood. Deuteronomy 21:6 (NIV) commands, "Then all the elders of the town nearest the body shall wash their hands – and they shall declare: Our hands did not shed this blood, nor did our eyes see it done. Accept this atonement for your people Israel, whom you have redeemed. Oh Lord, do not hold your people guilty of the blood of an innocent man."

In the New Testament, Pontius Pilate used the same custom of washing his hands concerning the death of Yeshua. "When Pilate saw that he (Pilate) was accomplishing nothing, but rather that a riot was starting, he took water, washed his hands in front of the crowd and said, 'My hands are clean of this man's blood'" (Matthew 27:24, CJB). Pilate used the Jewish custom of atonement for the shedding of innocent blood to announce that he was not guilty of Yeshua's unjust murder. Therefore, law and history unite in the washing of the hands.

Blessed are You, Adonai our God, King of the Universe, who has sanctified us by your commandments and has commanded us to wash our hands.

Baruch atah, Adonai Eloheinu, Melech haolam, asher bara et pri hagefen, shehecheyanu vakiymanu vahegianu lazman hazeh.

ברוך אתה אדוני אלוהינו , מלך העולם, אשר ברא את פרי הגפן, שהחיינו וקיימנו והגיענו לזמן הזה

The head of the household (hereafter, referred to as the Celebrant) washes his hands.

חי

The Invitation

The Haggadah begins with words of hope and promise. Our fathers knew affliction in Egypt, yet, they were redeemed. Redemption always remains available regardless of how difficult the situation. Since, we were once slaves and strangers in the land of Egypt, we invite the stranger, the hungry, and the oppressed to join us in the Passover festival. We remember that Yeshua said, "Come to me, all you who labor and are heavily burdened, and I will give you rest" (Matthew 11:28, WEB). This represents the bread of affliction which our ancestors ate in Egypt. Let those that are hungry come and eat. Let those that are oppressed share with us the hope of Passover. As we celebrate here, we join people everywhere.

Celebrant: At each place setting stands a wine glass to hold the four cups of wine used in the Seder meal. Fill each glass ½ full. Generally, the server at each table will refill the wine glasses as required during the Seder.

With four cups of wine, we recall each one of the promises by Adonai: the Cup of Sanctification, the Cup of Blessing and Promise, the Cup of Redemption, and the Cup of Acceptance. Wine symbolizes the joy that remains ours because of our ancestor's deliverance from Egypt. Passover retells Adonai's promise of freedom for our people.

Kiddush – The First Cup: The Cup of Sanctification

Celebrant: Hold up the first cup, the Cup of Sanctification.

The first cup is the Cup of Sanctification. Exodus 6:6 (WEB) says, "Therefore tell the children of Israel, 'I am Adonai and I will bring you out from under the burdens of the Egyptians, and I will rid you out of their bondage, and I will redeem you with outstretched arms, and with mighty acts of judgement. I will take you to Myself for a people." The promise of Adonai sets the Israelites apart from other nations and contains the hope that "I [Adonai] will take you from among the nations, gather you from all the countries and return you to your own soil" (Ezekiel 36:24, CJB).

As believers in Yeshua, we celebrate the same four promises of God. 1 Peter 1:18-19 (WEB) says, "knowing that you were redeemed, not with corruptible things, with silver or gold, from the useless way of life handed down from your fathers, but with precious blood, as of a lamb without blemish or spot, the blood of" Yeshua. Through faith in Yeshua, we are called to be set apart as children of Adonai.

Blessed is Adonai, King of the universe, who created the fruit of the Vine and who kept us in life, sustained us, and brought us to this festive season. Amen!

Baruch atah, Adonai Eloheinu, Melech haolam, asher bara et pri hagefen, shehecheyanu vakiymanu vahegianu lazman hazeh.

ברוך אתה אדוני אלוהינו, מלך העולם, אשר ברא את פרי הגפן, שהחיינו וקיימנו והגיענו לזמן הזה

Celebrant: Lift the Cup of Sanctification and say,

Let us partake of the first cup, the Cup of Sanctification.

Celebrant: All drink the first cup of wine.

Optional song: "Awesome God" by Rich Mullins (1988)

(Chorus only)

Our God is an awesome God

He reigns from heaven above

With wisdom, power, and love

Our God is an awesome God

Ma-Nishtanah – The Four Questions

Exodus 10:9 (NIV) says, "We will go with our young and old, with our sons and daughters, with our flocks and herds, because we are to celebrate a festival to" Adonai. To this day, our children continue to join in the Passover. Proverbs 22:6 (CJB) commands us to "Train a child in the way he should go; even when he is old, he will not swerve from it." Traditionally, the youngest child asks four questions. Today, we distributed the four questions to four different people (preferably four children). This keeps the children involved. Yeshua said in Matthew 19:14 (NIV), "Let the little children come to me and do not hinder them. For the kingdom of heaven belongs to such as these." Additionally, the children ask questions to give us the opportunity to retell the Passover Story – the story of our deliverance.

Child 1: Why is this night different from all other nights? On all other nights we eat either leavened bread or unleavened bread; on this night, why do we eat only unleavened bread? This night is different from other nights because tonight we celebrate the deliverance and redemption of the children of Adonai. We eat matzo to remember that in haste our ancestors left Egypt. Leaven is a substance that overtime causes dough to expand or grow. The Israelites did not have time to wait for the bread to rise (Exodus 12:39) so they ate unleavened bread.

Child 2: On all other nights, we eat all kinds of herbs. Why on this night do we eat bitter herbs? We eat bitter herbs to remember the bitterness of slavery that our ancestors experienced in Egypt. Exodus 1:14 (AMP) laments, "They made their lives bitter with hard labor in mortar, brick, and all kinds of field work. All their labor was harsh and severe."

Child 3: On all other nights, we do not dip our herbs at all. Why on this night do we dip them? Greens dipped in saltwater remind us of the tears of thankfulness that replaced the bitterness of slavery and death. The greens dipped in saltwater taste bitter to remind us of the sweetness of Adonai's mercy in rescuing us from death. Matthew 1:21 (CJB) further explains the mercy of Adonai by stating, "She [Mary] will give birth to a son and you are to name Him Yeshua, [which means Adonai saves] because He will save His people from their sins." Let us remember that slavery to sin always results in death, but due to Adonai's great mercy that we are saved from both slavery and death by His Son, *Yeshua HaMashiach*.

Child 4: On all other nights, we eat in an ordinary manner. Why tonight do we dine with special ceremony? Adonai made this meal special. When we first ate this meal in Egypt, Adonai rescued us from slavery and made us into a holy nation set apart for Him. We dine with special ceremony because we want to remember that only free men can relax while they eat.

Optional song: Dayenu

If He had brought us out from Egypt,

and had not carried out judgments against them - It would have sufficed!

אילו הוציאנו ממצרים

ולא עשה בהם שפטים – דיינו

Ilu hotzianu mimitzrayim

valo asah bahem sh'fatim – dayeinu

If He had carried out judgments against them,

and not against their idols - It would have sufficed!

אילו עשה בהם שפטים

ולא עשה באלהיהם – דיינו

Ilu asah bahem sh'fatim

v'lo asah beloheihem – dayeinu

It would have sufficed, It would have sufficed, It would have sufficed!

It would have sufficed, It would have sufficed, It would have sufficed!

די-דיינו, די-דיינו, די-דיינו, דיינו דיינו

דיינו די-דיינו, די-דיינו, די-דיינו, דיינו דיינו

Die-dayeinu, die-dayeinu, die-dayeinu, dayeinu dayeinu

*Dayeinu, die-dayeinu, die-dayeinu, die-dayeinu,
dayeinu dayeinu*

Maggid - The Story of Passover

Scripture commands us to tell our children about the exodus from Egypt. "This day shall be a memorial for you. You shall keep it as a feast to Adonai. You shall keep it as a feast throughout your generations by an ordinance forever." (Exodus 12:14, WEB). Thus, we repeat the Passover story. While the story remains ancient, the Passover story breathes new life each time we celebrate it. Our story moves from slavery toward freedom; it begins with degradation and rises to dignity. Our celebration opens with the rule of evil and advances toward the Kingdom of Adonai.

Long ago your ancestors lived in the land of Mesopotamia and worshipped other gods. Then Adonai called Abraham and lead him throughout the land of Canaan. Abraham had two sons, one of the sons was Isaac. Isaac beget two sons, Jacob and Esau. Over time, Jacob beget twelve sons. Joseph, one of Jacob's son, served Pharaoh. Joseph traveled throughout Egypt as pharaohs' second in command and oversaw the surplus food collection during the seven years of great harvest. Then, seven years of famine began. The famine became severe throughout the world, but in Egypt there was food. Joseph opened the storehouses and sold grain. People from other countries came to Egypt to buy grain (Genesis 41:53-57). Desperate for food, Jacob and his other sons came to live in northern Egypt in the region of Goshen.

Eventually Joseph, his father, his brothers, and all that generation died. Over the next four hundred years, the Israelite population grew. Then a new pharaoh, who did not know about Joseph, became ruler in Egypt. Pharaoh said to his people, "the Israelites have become far too numerous for us. Come, we must deal shrewdly with them or they will become even more numerous and, if war breaks out, will join our enemies, fight against us and leave the country." (Exodus 1:9-10, NIV). Subsequently, the Egyptians put slave masters over the Israelites to oppress them with forced labor. The more oppressive the Egyptians became, however, the more the Israelite population multiplied. The Egyptians despised the Israelites and made their lives bitter with hard, ruthless labor and all types of fieldwork (Exodus 1:11-16).

Meanwhile, the Israelites groaned in their slavery and cried out to Adonai. Adonai heard their weeping and remembered His covenant with Abraham, Isaac, and Jacob. Adonai looked on the Israelites and understood their concerns (Exodus 2:23-25). At the end of 430 years, the descendants of Jacob left Egypt. Adonai brought us out of Egypt with a mighty hand, outstretched arms, great terror, miraculous signs and wonders. For on that night Adonai passed through Egypt and struck down every first born: men and animals. Moreover, Adonai brought judgement on all the gods of Egypt (Exodus 12:12).

Today, we remember that Adonai passed over us when He saw the blood of the Passover lamb marking the doorposts. As commanded in Exodus 12:17, we celebrate this day the Passover of Adonai, the Feast of Unleavened Bread, as a lasting ordinance for the generations to come. We recite and demonstrate the Passover story. In front of me (*the Celebrant*) sits the Seder plate. Just like the Passover story, the different items on the Seder plate help us remember the significance of Passover.

Karpas – The Parsley

Celebrant: Hold up a sprig of parsley so that everyone can see it. Meanwhile, a sprig of parsley is given to each person.

We start with parsley - one of the first herbs of the new year. Parsley represents the new life given to the children of Israel. Saltwater represents: the many tears that the Israelites shed as slaves, the many tears we shed from our slavery to sins, and the sea that the children of Israel crossed. By dipping the parsley into the saltwater, we remember that Adonai saved the Israelites when He brought them safely through the sea and made them into a new nation.

We know that the new life offered by Yeshua comes only after tears of repentance. Paul writes in 1 Corinthians 10:1 (WEB) that "I would not have you ignorant, brothers, that our fathers were all under the cloud, and all passed through the sea; and were all baptized into Moses in the cloud and in the sea; and all ate the same spiritual food; and all drank the same spiritual drink. For they drank of a spiritual rock that followed them, and the rock was Christ." Acts 4:12 teaches that Yeshua (meaning Adonai saves) remains the only way for salvation, there exists nothing or anyone, be it person or deity, through which a person can receive salvation.

Let us pray, blessed are You, Adonai our God, King of the Universe, who has created the fruit of the earth and has given us the way to salvation. Amen!

Baruch atah, Adonai Eloheinu, Melech haolam, asher bara et pri haaretz, venatan lanu et haderekh layashua. Amen.

ברוך אתה אדוני אלוהינו , מלך העולם, אשר ברא את פרי הארץ ונתן לנו את הדרך לישועה. אמן.

Now, we may eat the parsley dipped in saltwater.

Matzo – The Bread

Celebrant: Momentarily hold a piece of matzo up where all can see it.

Matzo consists only of flour and water. Consequently, matzo does not ferment or sour. Matzo reminds us that on the night when Adonai delivered the children of Israel from Egypt, they left in such a great hurry that the dough had no time to rise before it baked. Exodus 12:33-34 conveys that the Egyptians desperately wanted the Israelites to leave; this promoted the Israelites to wrap unleavened bread dough in clean cloth and place the unleavened dough into kneading troughs. Thus, prophecy and history meet in that the true bread of life, Yeshua, also was wrapped in swaddling cloth and laid in a trough.

Adonai commanded that for eight days we abstain from leaven. Leaven depicts what moral corruption, evil, or sin does to our lives. Moral corruption festers and grows. Just as there remains no quantity of leaven in the matzo, sin should not be tolerated in our lives. The slightest quantity of leaven remains forbidden because it eventually spoils the bread. 1 Corinthians 5:7-8 (AMP) demands that we "Clean out the old leaven so that you may be a new batch, just as you are, still unleavened. For Christ our Passover Lamb has been sacrificed. Therefore, let us celebrate the feast, not with old leaven, nor with leaven of vice and malice and wickedness, but with the unleavened bread of sincerity and truth." We are called to be set apart from sin (1 Corinthians 1:2).

The matzo presents an exceptional comparison to Yeshua. Just as bread acted as a nutritious, life sustaining food for the Israelites, the Bread of Life, Yeshua, prevails as a life-giving source for the believer. Yeshua proclaimed in John 6:35 (CJB), "I am the bread of life. Whoever comes to Me will never go hungry, and whoever trusts in Me will never be thirsty."

Let us examine the matzo. First, just as the matzo remains without leaven; so Yeshua remained without sin. Second, the matzo was pierced with a pointed instrument to keep it from bubbling under the flame. Similarly, nails and a spear pierced Yeshua. Psalm 22:16 (WEB) prophesizes that "they have pierced my hands and feet." Zechariah 12:10 (WEB) prophesizes, "They will look to me whom they have pierced." Again, prophecy and history meet at Yeshua's crucifixion when the soldiers came to Yeshua and observed that He was dead, the soldiers did not break his legs like they had the other individuals crucified with Yeshua. However, a soldier stabbed Yeshua with a spear (John 19:32-34). Third, the holes in the matzo create stripes across the back of the matzo. In the same way, by mocking, beating, and imbedding a crown of thrones on Yeshua head, the soldiers wounded Yeshua. Isaiah 53:5 (WEB) affirms, "He was pierced for our transgression. He was crushed for our iniquities. The punishment that brought our peace was on Him; and by His wounds we are healed."

Celebrant: Lift the three matzos together in the cloth.

I hold three matzos wrapped up together in a single, clean, white linen cloth that symbolizes our relationship with God. The top matzo symbolizes Adonai. Traditionally, the center piece of matzo represents the mediating high priest between Adonai and man. As believers in Yeshua, we understand that Yeshua is the ultimate high priest - the bridge between Adonai and man.

Yeshua stands in the place of intercession and sacrificial atonement. Subsequently, Yeshua was slaughtered, wrapped in linen, and hidden in a tomb. The center matzo represents *Yeshua HaMashiach,* Jesus the Messiah. The third piece of matzo represents us, the believer in the God of Abraham, Isaac and Jacob and in His only begotten son, Yeshua. In the Old Testament, we are reminded that Adonai "humbled you, allowed you to be hungry, and fed you with manna, which you didn't know, neither did your fathers know, that He might teach you that man does not live by bread only, but man lives by every word that proceeds out of" the mouth of Adonai (Deuteronomy 8:3, WEB).

Celebrant: Take the uppermost of the three matzos and then break it into the number of pieces that you have guests. Place the number of pieces on a plate. Each person takes one piece. Hold the matzo so that all individuals can partake together.

Let us pray. Blessed are You, Adonai, King of the universe, who brings forth bread from the earth. Amen.

Baruch atah, Adonai Eloheinu, Melech haolam, hamotzia lechem min haaretz. Amen.

ברוך אתה אדוני אלוהינו, מלך העולם, המוציא לחם מן הארץ. אמן.

We now share the piece of matzo.

Celebrant: Everyone eats the piece of matzo.

Yachutz – Breaking the Middle Matzo

Now, we break the middle piece of matzo in half. Traditionally, the middle matzo is broken because Adonai instructed Abraham to offer a heifer, ram, goat, dove, and young pigeon splitting them in half as a sacrifice to Adonai (Genesis 15:9). The breaking or splitting of the center matzo represents the blood sacrifice and the splitting of the animals by Abraham and the beginning of the Abrahamic covenant. Additionally, within the Mosaic covenant, the matzo represents redemption. While the Israelites were redeemed from slavery in Egypt, they anticipate the ultimate redemption through Messiah. Hiding the middle matzo symbolized the belief that Messiah will come to redeem the nation.

The middle matzo is the afikomen - a Greek word *(epikomion)* that means 'after the banquet'. Appropriately, the middle piece of matzo will be eaten after the banquet. Until that time, the middle piece remains hidden because Yeshua remained hidden from us for three days after He died. As the head of the house, I will hide the broken pieces and the children will search for the afikomen after the meal. They need to pay close attention to be able to discover where the afikomen lays hidden.

Celebrant: Take the matzo and break the middle piece in half and then wrap both halves in one linen cloth and hide it. Often, the Celebrant secretly hands the afikomen to another person or the woman of the house to hide.

Optional song: O Come, O Come Emmanuel by JM Neale (1861 translation)

> *O come, o come, Emmanuel,*
>
> *And ransom captive Israel,*
>
> *That mourns in lonely exile here*
>
> *Until the Son of God appear.*
>
> *Rejoice! Rejoice! Emmanuel*
>
> *Shall come to thee, O Israel.*

Maror – The Bitter Herb (Horseradish)

Horseradish tastes bitter and symbolizes the bitterness of slavery. Horseradish brings a tear to the eye, just as the children of Israel cried out with anguish to Adonai against their taskmasters. We eat bitter herbs to remember that the Egyptians embittered the lives of our people. Exodus 1:14 (NIV) explains, the Egyptians "made their lives bitter with hard labor in brick and mortar and with all kinds of work in the fields; in all their hard labor the Egyptians used them ruthlessly". Sin persists as a harsh taskmaster that pays its subjects with death. Romans 6:23 (WEB) announces that penalty of sin is death.

The bitter herb carried on the back of the matzo, reminds us that Yeshua carried the bitterness of our slavery to sin onto the cross. During Yeshua's crucifixion, He offered Himself in place of our sins (1 Peter 2:24) so that we could be redeemed from the penalty of sin (Romans 6:23). Isaiah 43:25 expounds that our sin and offenses disgust Adonai. We are reminded to acknowledge and profess our sins to Adonai and proclaim that He can surround us songs of deliverance (Psalm 32:5-7).

A pinch of horseradish placed on a bite-size piece of matzo to remind us of our deliverance from Egypt.

Celebrant: Server takes bit-sized pieces of matzo, one for each person, and places a pinch of horseradish on each matzo. Place the matzo/horseradish on a plate. Wait until all individuals have a sample, then partake together.

Charoseth

Charoseth consists of a mixture of coarsely chopped apples, nuts and raisins mixed in honey and grape juice. It resembles, in appearance, the mortar used by the children of Israel to make bricks in Egypt. Thus, charoseth reminds us of the harsh taskmasters, the bricks that the Israelites made, and the mortar used to hold those bricks together.

Again, a pinch of horseradish rests on a bite-sized piece of matzo. This time, enough charoseth is added to remove the sting of the horseradish. In this, we demonstrate that even during trials we hope in Adonai's deliverance, knowing God's grace continues despite adversity. Also, Yeshua carried the bitterness and weight of our sins on the cross.

Celebrant: Use individual bite size matzo or break large matzo into the number of pieces to accommodate everyone. Place a pinch of horseradish on each piece of matzo and cover the horseradish with a dollop of charoseth. Place the horseradish / charoseth matzo on a plate and pass. Wait until everyone has a piece and then partake together.

The Passover Lamb – The Shank Bone

This shank bone is symbolic of the slain Passover lamb. To protect themselves from death, the Israelites killed a one-year-old male lamb without spot or blemish as instructed. Then, they dipped hyssops into the lamb's blood, struck the upper lintel, and the two side posts of the front door at the place where they ate the Passover meal. This significant prophetic action outlines the shape of the cross drawn with the Passover lamb's blood.

Ironically, hyssop is a plant from the mint family that grows to be three to four feet long. In Egypt, hyssop was commonly used for cleaning. This night hyssop was used to cleanse the household from death. Exodus 12:13 (AMP) says, "The blood shall be a sign for you on [the doorposts of] the houses where you live; when I see the blood I shall pass over you, and no affliction shall happen to you to destroy you when I strike the land of Egypt." Thus, Adonai passed over the Israelites and did not strike the first-born dead during the tenth and final plague. About 2,500 years later, Yeshua was sacrificed on a cross outside of Jerusalem. The true Passover lamb, Yeshua, shed His blood to redeem us, the believers, from death.

You may ask, why did the Israelites need protection from the judgement of Adonai? Scripture affirms that "There is not a righteous man on earth who always does good and who never sins" (Ecclesiastes 7:20, AMP) and the person "who sins, he shall die" (Ezekiel 18:20, WEB). Every man, woman, and child fail to uphold the law of Adonai. The blood of an innocent lamb became the symbol of the innocent life used to redeem the children of Israel from the judgement of Adonai. Exodus 12:12-13 warns that Adonai would go throughout the land of Egypt and kill every firstborn of man and animal and pass judgments against all Egyptian gods. Yet, the blood of the Passover lamb smeared on the doorposts of the Israelite houses allowed Adonai to pass over the house so that the plague would not affect those inside the Israelite house.

Again, prophecy and history meet. Paul confirms, "Christ, our Passover Lamb, has been sacrificed" (1 Corinthians 5:7, AMP). Isaiah prophesied, Yeshua "was oppressed, yet when He was afflicted, He didn't open His mouth. As a lamb that is led to the slaughter, and as a sheep that before its shearers is silent, so he didn't open his mouth" (Isaiah 53:7, WEB). John the Baptist proclaimed, "Behold, the Lamb of God, who takes away the sin of the world" (John 1:29, WEB). Through Yeshua, death passes over the believer. By the blood of the Passover lamb, the Israelites lived. Salvation endures, even today, through the blood of the Passover Lamb, Yeshua.

The Ten Plagues

Exodus 9:13-14 (WEB) records that Moses spoke to Pharaoh announcing, Adonai says, "Let my people go, that they may serve me … that you may know that there is no one like Me in all the earth." Adonai sent ten plagues upon the Egyptians. Wine symbolizes the blood of the Passover lamb poured out as our sacrifice and protective covering. Leviticus 17:11 (NIV) clarifies the importance of the blood, "for the life of a creature is in the blood, and I have given it to you to make atonement for yourselves on the altar; it is the blood that makes atonement for one's life." By the blood of the Passover Lamb, we received forgiveness of sins.

The plagues fulfilled two purposes. The first purpose revealed Adonai's power and the offer of salvation to the Israelites. The second purpose showed Adonai's superiority over all the gods of Egypt. Egypt was a polytheistic society meaning that they had many gods. Through the plagues, Adonai displayed His extreme power over the Egyptian gods. Since we do not want to partake in any of the ten plagues, we remove one drop of wine by dipping our little finger into the wine for each of the plagues and wiping the wine drop on our napkin.

Celebrant: You can distribute the reading of the ten plagues between different people in attendance. This allows others to actively participate in the celebration. (Due to time constraints, it is optional to only read the names of the plagues. If selecting this option say 'Symbolically, let us take a drop of wine out of our glass and wipe it on our napkin as I read the names of the plagues so that we do not partake in the plagues.')

The first plague – blood, *Dahm*

The second plague – frogs, *Tzfardeyah*

The third plague – gnats, *Kinim*

The fourth plague – beetles, *Arov*

The fifth plague – pestilence, *Dever*

The sixth plague – boils, *Sh'him*

The seventh plague - hail, *Barad*

The eighth plague - locust, *Arbeh*

The ninth plague – darkness, *Hosheh*

The tenth plague – slaying of the first born, *Makat B'horot*

The First Plague – Blood, *Dahm*

Adonai declared in Exodus 7:19 (WEB), "Tell Aaron, 'Take your rod, and stretch out your hand over the waters of Egypt, over their rivers, over their streams, and over their pools, and over all their ponds of water, that they may become blood. There will be blood throughout all the land of Egypt, both in vessels of wood and in vessels of stone.'" Geographically, the Nile River comprised the main trade route through Egypt. Trade, commerce and agriculture depended directly on the water of the Nile River. The plague of blood killed the fish in the Nile, navigation stagnated, surface water became undrinkable; Egypt entered an acute health and economic crisis without access to water.

This plague directly confronted many Egyptian gods, Khnum, the guardian of the Nile River did not respond. Hapi, the dynamic essence of the Nile, the lord of the fish, birds and marshes remained useless. Nu, the deity that Egyptians believed created the world, the god of life, the maker and molder of the universe stood powerless. Osiris, the god of the afterlife, the god whom Egyptians believed possessed the Nile River as his bloodstream, one of the greatest and most powerful of all Egyptian gods, was silent. The Egyptian gods connected to the Nile River were unequal to the superiority of Adonai. Thus, by the plague of blood, Adonai let the Egyptians people know that "I am Adonai, and there is no other; besides Me there is no God" (Isaiah 45:5, CJB).

Symbolically, let us take a drop of wine out of our glass and wipe it on our napkin so that we do not partake in the plague of blood.

חי

The Second Plague – Frogs, *Tzfardeyah*

Exodus 8:3 (WEB) affirms, "The [Nile] river will swarm with frogs, which will go up and come into your house, and into your bedroom, and on your bed, and into the house of your servants, and on your people, and into your ovens, and into your kneading troughs." Thus, literally, frogs were everywhere.

By Egyptian law, the frog was sacred and involuntarily killing frogs was punishable by death. Religiously, the frog represented the physical manifestation of the deity Hept - goddess of childbirth and wife of the creator of the world. Egyptian women found it fashionable to wear jewelry with the frog image as a sign of their devotion. The eight frog/serpent deity circle of the Ogdoad was also addressed. Egyptians believed that the Ogdoad Council consisted of the male and female personifications for the creation waters, space, darkness, and invisibility. The second plague showed Adonai's dominion over Heqt and the Ogdoad Council. Therefore, through the plague of frogs, Adonai let the Egyptians know that Adonai created the heavens and established the earth to be inhabited and teaming with life (Isaiah 45:18). Adonai says, "I am Adonai, and there is no other" (Isaiah 45:5, CJB).

Today, we know Adonai brings life. Jeremiah 1:5 (WEB) proclaims, "Before I formed you in the womb, I knew you. Before you were born, I sanctified you." As for the beginning of the universe, Genesis 1:1-4 (WEB) declares, "God created the heavens and the earth. The earth was formless and empty. Darkness was on the surface of the deep and God's Spirit was hovering over the surface of the waters. God said, 'Let there be light,' and there was light. God saw the light and saw that it was good. God divided the light from the darkness." Thus, creation belongs to the dominion of Adonai, not to the Ogdoad Council.

Symbolically, let us take a drop of wine out of our glass and wipe it on our napkin so that we do not partake in the plague of frogs.

The Third Plague – Gnats, *Kinim*

Then Adonai spoke to Moses, "Stretch out your staff and strike the dust of the ground,' and throughout the land of Egypt the dust will become gnats" (Exodus 8:16, NIV). Subsequently, the gnats, a tiny biting insect infested both people and animals. The significance of the gnats refers to where they live – the dust became gnats. The Egyptian god of dirt was Geb. His physical manifestation resembled a man. The Egyptians believed that Geb held the souls of the wicked so that the wicked could not enter paradise.

Adonai holds everything in heaven and earth. Isaiah 40:12 (WEB) further explains that Adonai holds "the dust of the earth in a measuring basket," not Geb. 1 Samuel 2:8 (NIV) confirms, "the foundations of the earth are the LORD'S." Today, we understand that Yeshua, the Passover Lamb, will judge the living and the dead, not Geb. 1 Peter 4:5 (WEB) attests that "They will give account to Him who is ready to judge the living and the dead." There is not a debate between the greatness of Adonai and the Egyptian deity, Geb. Geb remained silent. Domain over the earth belongs to Adonai for Isaiah 45:5 (CJB) vows, "I am Adonai, and there is no other; besides Me there is no God".

Symbolically, let us take a drop of wine out of our glass and wipe it on our napkin so that we do not partake in the plague of gnats.

The Fourth Plague – Beetles, *Arov*

Remember, the purpose of the ten plagues revealed Adonai's power to the Israelites and showed Adonai's superiority over all the gods of Egypt. Exodus 9:14 (WEB) affirms Adonai's purpose in that "you may know that there is no one like Me in all the earth." Thus, Adonai directed the fourth plague.

Incidentally, the translation into English from the original Hebrew in later centuries translated the fourth plague as of flies. According to the original Hebrew, the fourth plague was a plague of beetles. Exodus 8:21-24 (YLT) declares, "I am sending against you, and against your servants, and against your people, and against your house, the beetle. The houses and ground of the Egyptians will be full of the beetle. I will separate on that day the land of Goshen, in which My people are staying, that the beetle is not there, so that you know that I [am] Adonai in the midst of the land, and I have put a division between My people and your people. Then Adonai did so, and the grievous beetle entered the house of Pharaoh, and the house of his servants, and in all the land of Egypt the land was corrupted from the presence of the beetle."

Why is the beetle verses the fly important? To the Egyptians, the beetle personified the god Khepri, yet the fly remained simply an insect. The Egyptian god Khepri existed as a creator-god that pushed the sun across the sky each day. The physical manifestation of Khepri resembled the scarab beetle. Often, the scarab beetle's image seals official documents and decorate lids and wine jars. Jewelry made in the shape of the scarab beetle functions as a protective amulet or fetish.

Adonai stated, "I am Adonai, and there is no other; besides Me there is no God" (Isaiah 45:5, CJB). Today, we understand that the worship of animals that crawl upon the ground remains an abomination to Adonai. Deuteronomy 4:15-19 (WEB) admonishes, "Be very careful ... lest you corrupt yourselves, and make yourself a carved image in the form of any figure, the likeness of male or female, the likeness of any animal that is on the earth, the likeness of any winged bird that flies in the sky, the likeness of anything that creeps on the ground, the likeness of any fish that is in the water under the earth; and lest you lift up your eyes to the sky, and when you see the sun and the moon and the stars, even all the army of the sky, you are drawn away and worship them, and serve them." Adonai brought the Israelites out of Egypt to be a nation that Adonai created not Khepri. Isaiah 40:28 (NIV) proclaims, Adonai "is the everlasting God, the Creator of the ends of the earth."

Symbolically, let us take a drop of wine out of our glass and wipe it on our napkin so that we do not partake in the plague of beetles.

The Fifth Plague – Pestilence on Livestock, *Dever*

Moses warned Pharaoh, "If you refuse to let [the Israelites] go and continue to hold back, the hand of the LORD will bring a terrible plague upon your livestock in the field – on your horses and donkeys and camels and on your cattle and sheep and goats" (Exodus 9:2-3, NIV). With the plague upon livestock, Adonai made a marked separation between Israelite and Egyptian cattle. This plague only killed the livestock in the fields belonging to Egyptians. Because of the plague's severity, Pharaoh sent investigators to see if any Israelite livestock died. The investigators reported, "not so much as one of the livestock of the Israelites died" (Exodus 9:7, WEB).

The fifth plague rails against two of the main Egyptian animal deities, Ptah and Hathor, and a score of minor animal deities. Egyptians believed that livestock represented the living image of many Egyptian deities. Apis, the bull, was worshiped as the living image of the creator god, Ptah. Credited with creating man's body in the afterlife, the Egyptians believed that Ptah created the heavens and the earth. Appropriately, Adonai dethrones Ptah because Genesis 1:1 (WEB) assert, "In the beginning God created the heavens and the earth", not Ptah.

Hathor's living representation was a cow. Considered the sky goddess or queen of heaven, Hathor co-ruled over the dead. Egyptians believed that Hathor gave comfort to the dead by providing food and drink for people who found shade under her sacred tree of life. Hathor was a fertility goddess; ceremonies performed in her temple were laden with debauchery. Today, worldwide worship of Hathor exists in most cultures, but she uses the cultural names associated with the queen of heaven.

As believers, we are commanded not to partake in the worship of Hathor, queen of heaven. Proverbs 23:20-21 (WEB) teaches, "Don't be among ones drinking too much wine, or those who gorge themselves on meat: for drunkards and gluttons shall become poor." 1 Peter 4:3-5 (NIV) imparts, "we have spent enough of our past time doing the desire of the Gentiles, and having walked in lewdness, lusts, drunken binges, orgies, carousing's, and abominable idolatries. They think it is strange that you don't run with them into the same excess of riot, blaspheming. They will give account to Him who is ready to judge the living and the dead."

In Stephen's speech before the Sanhedrin (Acts 7), Stephen quoted Adonai through the prophet Amos (Amos 5:27) denouncing Hebrew construction and worship of idols. Idolatry is a violation of the first commandment. Today, the ramifications of idolatry and worship of the queen of heaven remains an abomination to Adonai. Adonai declared in Isaiah 45:5 (CJB), "I am Adonai, and there is no other; besides Me there is no God". May we as believers never worship the queen of heaven.

Let us take a drop of wine out of our glass and wipe it on our napkin so that we do not partake in the plague of pestilence on livestock.

The Sixth Plague – Boils, *Sh'him*

Exodus 9:8-9 (WEB) notes that Adonai spoke to Moses and Aaron commanding, 'Take handfuls of ashes from the furnace, and let Moses sprinkle it toward the sky in the sight of Pharaoh. It shall become small dust over all the land of Egypt and shall be boils and blisters breaking out on men and on animals throughout all the land of Egypt." Deuteronomy 28:35 expands our understanding that the boils affected anywhere from the bottom of their feet to the top of their head.

The Egyptian god, Imhotep, was originally a physician and advisor to the ruler Zoser (about 3,150 BC). Imhotep became the Egyptian god of medicine due to the discoveries and advances that Imhotep made in Egyptian medicine. Imhotep was the Egyptian deity over knowledge, science, and the arts. The sixth plague confronted the Egyptian medical deity.

Psalms 103:2-4 (WEB) instructs us to praise Adonai "and don't forget all his benefits, who forgives all your sins, who heals all your diseases, who redeems your life from destruction." Therefore, Adonai heals, not Imhotep. While

Yeshua was on earth, Yeshua healed people with "various diseases and torments, possessed with demons, epileptics, and paralytics" (Matthew 4:24, WEB). Thus, healing does not come from the Egyptian deity, Imhotep, but from Adonai. As Isaiah 45:5 (CJB) emphasizes, "I am Adonai, and there is no other; besides Me there is no God".

Symbolically, let us take a drop of wine out of our glass and wipe it on our napkin so that we do not partake in the plague of boils.

The Seventh Plague – Hail, *Barad*

Adonai told Moses to confront Pharaoh saying, "Let My people go, that they may serve Me. For this time, I will send all My plagues against your heart, against your officials, and against your people; that you may know that there is no one like Me in all the earth. For now I would have stretched out My hand, and struck you and your people with pestilence, and you would have been cut off from the earth; but indeed for this cause I have made you stand: to show you My power, and that My name may be declared throughout all the earth, because you still exalt yourself against My people, that you won't let them go. Behold, tomorrow about this time I will cause it to rain a very grievous hail, such as has not been in Egypt since the day it was founded even until now. Now therefore command that all your livestock and all that you have in the field be brought into shelter. The hail will come down on every man and animal that is found in the field, and isn't brought home, and they will die" (Exodus 9:13-20, WEB).

Scientifically, hail is associated with the sky, particularly, severe thunderstorms. The seventh plague assaults the Egyptian deities: Min and Nut. As a fertility god, Min visually represents the fertile Nile soil. Min resided in the surrounding Egyptian desert; he rumbled with necessary rain via the thunderbolt. Personified in a bedazzlement of stars and celestial bodies, Nut endures as the mother of Osiris – Egyptian god of resurrection and eternal life.

Today, the ramifications of idolatry and the deity worship of Nut and many livestock deities remain an abomination to Adonai. Adonai affirms in Isaiah 45:5 (CJB), "I am Adonai, and there is no other; besides Me there is no God".

Symbolically let us take a drop of wine out of our glass and wipe it on our napkin that we do not partake in the plague of hail.

חי

The Eighth Plague – Locust, *Arbeh*

Adonai instructs Moses to tell pharaoh "Tomorrow I (Adonai) will bring locusts into your country, and they shall cover the surface of the earth, so that one won't be able to see the earth. They shall eat the residue of that which has escaped, which remains to you from the hail, and shall eat every tree which grows for you out of the field. Your houses shall be filled, and the houses of all your servants, and the houses of all the Egyptians, as neither your fathers nor your fathers' fathers have seen, since the day that they were on the earth to this day" (Exodus 10:4-6, WEB).

The eighth plague brought the destruction of living vegetation in Egypt for all green vegetation was eaten by the locusts (Exodus 10:15). Egypt's major deity for grain became useless in preserving their domain against Adonai. Through this plague, Adonai mightily showed His power over Osiris. By tradition, Egyptians believed that Osiris traveled the whole world and taught men to cultivate fruit, vegetables, and grains. Greatly respected as a grain god, Egyptians believed Osiris presided over the death and resurrection of plants, as well as, the death and resurrection of each person.

On the contrary, Deuteronomy 32:39 (NIV) admonishes that Adonai brings life, "I [Adonai] put to death and I bring to life, I have wounded and I will heal." The New Testament expounds on the topic of who controls life and death. Yeshua announced in John 5:24 (WEB), "He who hears My word and believes Him who sent Me has eternal life, and doesn't come into judgement, but has passed out of death into life." For the person who believes in the Lordship of Yeshua, there is eternal life. Thus, Osiris remains silent over issues of death and eternal life, but Adonai speaks.

Today, we know that Osiris does not hold the keys of death. Yeshua encourages the apostle John in Revelation 1:17-19 (NIV), "Do not be afraid. I am the First and the Last. I am the Living One; I was dead, and now look, I am alive for ever and ever! And I hold the keys of death and Hades." Let us remember that Adonai declares that, "I am Adonai, and there is no other; besides Me there is no God" (Isaiah 45:5, CJB).

Symbolically, let us take a drop of wine out of our glass and wipe it on our napkin so that we do not partake in the plague of locust.

חי

The Ninth Plague – Darkness, *Hosheh*

Exodus 10:21-22 (WEB) acknowledged that Adonai instructed Moses, "'Stretch out your hand toward the sky, that there may be darkness over the land of Egypt, even darkness which may be felt.' Moses stretched out his hand toward the sky, and there was a thick darkness in all the land of Egypt for three days." This plague assaulted the sun god, Re. To the Egyptians, life depended on the sun. Ironically, the sun god segmented into multiple deities/titles dependent upon the location of the sun. Egyptians believed that Re-created himself and all creation, that Re originated as a serpent, eventually took on human shape, and at the end of the world Re will revert to his original serpent shape.

First, Genesis describes the creation of the universe: light, dark, land, water, sky, dry ground, celestial bodies, plants, and animals. Adonai points out that He created it. Isaiah 45:12 (WEB) contends, "I have made the earth, and created man on it. I, even my hands, have stretched out the heavens." The darkness of the ninth plague proved the power of Adonai over light and darkness.

Secondly, the serpent tempted Eve in the Garden of Eden. Genesis 3:1-5 (WEB) reports, "Did God really said, 'You shall not eat of any tree in the garden?'... 'for God knows that in the day you eat it, your eyes will be opened, and you will be like God, knowing good and evil.'" After this statement from the serpent, Eve sinned by eating the fruit. Thus, the serpent put separation between mankind and Adonai. The first messianic prophecy follows the curse upon the serpent. Genesis 3:15 (WEB) imparts that "I [Adonai] will put hostility between you and the woman, and between your [serpent] offspring and her offspring; He [Yeshua] will bruise your head, and you will bruise His heel." Thus, with the ninth plague Adonai addressed the Egyptian deity Re.

Finally, the ninth plague was total darkness. Considering this event happened once in Egypt, could it ever happen again? Both the prophet Joel 2:31-32 (NIV) and the Acts 2:19-21 (NIV) emphasized that "The sun will be turned to darkness and the moon to blood before the coming of the great and terrible day of Adonai" (Joel 3:4,

CJB). So, when is the great and terrible Day of the Adonai? Revelation 6:12-13 (WEB) elaborates "I watched as he [Yeshua] opened the sixth seal and there was a great earthquake. The sun became black as sackcloth made of hair; the whole moon became as blood. The stars of the sky fell to the earth, like a fig tree dropping its unripe figs when it is shaken by a great wind." Therefore, if Adonai addressed Re once, could not Adonai address the issue again? What would you do if the sun turned black? Would you call upon the name of Adonai?

Today let us remember that there are no reasons anyone needs to stumble in darkness for, "The people who walked in darkness have seen a great light. The light has shined on those living in the land of the shadow of death" (Isaiah 9:2, WEB). Adonai again reminds us that, "besides Me there is no God" (Isaiah 45:5, CJB). Yes, Adonai prevails as LORD of the light and darkness.

Symbolically, let us take a drop of wine out of our glass and wipe it on our napkin so that we do not partake in the plague of darkness.

חי

The Tenth Plague – Slaying of the Firstborn, *Makat B'horot*

Moses announced, Adonai says, "About midnight I will go into the middle of Egypt and all the firstborn in the land of Egypt shall die, from the firstborn son of Pharaoh who sits on his throne, even to the firstborn of the female servant who is behind the mill, and all the firstborn of livestock. There will be a great cry throughout all the land of Egypt, such as there has not been, nor will be any more. But against any of the children of Israel a dog won't even bark or move its tongue, against man or animal, that you may know that the Adonai makes a distinction between Egyptians and Israel" (Exodus 11:4-7, WEB).

The plague of the death of the firstborn ranked as the most personally destructive and selective plague of all ten plagues for it would affect only the firstborn from Pharaoh's son, to the firstborn of the Egyptian slaves, to the firstborn of the remaining Egyptian owned livestock. Without exception, this plague directly assaulted all the gods of Egypt. Remember, Egypt existed as a polytheistic society. However, against the tenth plague, the Egyptian deities were powerless. As Adonai acknowledges in Isaiah 45:5 (CJB), "I am Adonai, and there is no other; besides Me there is no God".

There exists one SIGNIFICANT statement that should not be glossed over, "The blood will be a sign for you on the houses where you are; and when I see the blood, I (Adonai) will pass over you" (Exodus 12:13, NIV). The blood of the Passover lamb spared the children of Israel from the death of the firstborn. 1 Peter 1:18-19 (WEB) explains, "you were redeemed, not with corruptible things, with silver or gold, from the useless way of life handed down from your fathers, but with precious blood, as of a lamb without blemish or spot, the blood of Christ." The blood of the Passover lamb redeemed the Israelites from death. Likewise, the blood of the Passover Lamb, Yeshua, redeems us, the believers, from eternal death.

Tradition teaches that the blood of the lamb was placed on the door in such a way as to make a cross. Thus, over two thousand years prior to the actual crucifixion of Yeshua, the blood of the Passover lamb on the door frame of the houses for the Israelites allowed Adonai to pass over their homes. The thought that a simple cross could redeem people from death continues as unreasonable or foolish to many people. Yet, 1 Corinthians 1:18 (WEB) reaffirms, "For the word of the cross is foolishness to those who are dying, but to us who are being saved it is the power of" Adonai.

Symbolically, let us take a drop of wine out of our glass and wipe it on our napkin so that we do not partake in the plague of death.

Optional Song: And It Came to Pass at Midnight

> *In the days of old you performed many miracles at night.*
>
> *In the early watch of evening, on this night.*
>
> *To gain the victory, Abraham divided his army at night. (Genesis 14:15)*
>
> *And it came to pass at midnight.*
>
> *You judged Abimelech, king of Gerar, in a dream during the night; (Genesis 20:3)*
>
> *You struck Laban, the Syrian, with terror in the night; (Genesis 20:3)*

Israel wrestled with an angel and prevailed at night. (Genesis 32:25)

And it came to pass at midnight.

Egypt's first-born you smote at night;
(Exodus 12:29)

The Egyptians found themselves powerless when they arose at night.

You scattered Sisera's army, aided by the stars of night. (Judges 5:20)

It came to pass a midnight.

חי

The Second Cup: The Cup of Freedom

Celebrant: Take the cup of wine and hold it up until the prayer

With the ten drops of wine missing from the Cup of Freedom, also called the Cup of Blessing and Promise, we partake of the second cup. Traditionally, the Cup of Blessing and Promise represents the day the Israelites left Egypt – the first day of Blessing and Promise without enslavement. Exodus 6:6 (WEB) reveals, "Therefore tell the children of Israel, 'I am Adonai, and I will bring you out from under the burdens of the Egyptians, and I will rid you out of their bondage, and I will redeem you with an outstretched arm, and with great judgments.'" By Moses' outstretched arm, Adonai parted the sea as the last step toward the deliverance of His people from Egypt. Again, prophecy and history meet in that the very act of crucifixion requires an outstretched arm.

Psalm 24:1-6 (WEB) affirms, "The earth is Adonai's, with its fullness; the world, and those who dwell in it. For he has founded it on the seas and established it on the floods. Who may ascend to Adonai's hill? Who may stand in his holy place? He who has clean hands and a pure heart; who has not lifted up his soul to falsehood and has not sworn deceitfully. He shall receive a blessing from Yahweh, righteousness from the God of his salvation. This is the generation of those who seek Him, who seek your face." Drop by drop, sin by sin, we are called to remove sin from our lives for Adonai called us to be a royal people, a holy people.

We praise You, Adonai, who keeps faith with the people. We are privileged to praise, glorify, honor, exalt, and thank Adonai for the miracles brought to our ancestors that liberated them from the bondage of slavery in Egypt. Thank you for bringing us from sorrow to joy, from mourning to laughing, from darkness to a great light. Adonai's promise of freedom in ancient days sustains us even today.

Anachnu mahelelim otach, Adonai, asher nishaar neeman lam. Zcoatenu he lehalel, lekhabed velehudot leadonai al hanisim shchalu al avotinu asher shichreru otam mavdot bemitzrim. Toda lecha al hovaltenu miagon

le osher, me evel letzchokh, mechoshech leor adir. Havtachat Adonai lechirotf bayamim hakdomim mechazeket otanu ad hayiom.

אנחנו מהללים אותך אדוני, אשר נשאר נאמן לעם. זכותנו היא להלל, לכבד ולהודות לאדוני על הניסים שחלו על אבותינו אשר שחררו אותם מעבדות במצרים. תודה לך על הובלתנו מיגון לאושר, מאבל לצחוק, מחושך לאור אדיר. הבטחת אדוני לחירות בימים הקדומים מחזקת אותנו עד יהיום.

Celebrant: All drink the second cup of wine.

Optional Song: Psalm 136 (WEB)

> *Give thanks to Adonai, for he is good;*
> *for his loving kindness endures forever.*
> *Give thanks to the God of gods;*
> *for his loving kindness endures forever.*
> *Give thanks to the Lord of lords;*
> *for his loving kindness endures forever:*
> *to him who alone does great wonders;*
> *for his loving kindness endures forever:*

to him who by understanding made the heavens;

for his loving kindness endures forever:

to him who spread out the earth above the waters;

for his loving kindness endures forever:

to him who made the great lights;

for his loving kindness endures forever:

the sun to rule by day;

for his loving kindness endures forever;

the moon and stars to rule by night;

for his loving kindness endures forever:

to him who struck down the Egyptian firstborn;

for his loving kindness endures forever;

and brought out Israel from among them;

for his loving kindness endures forever;

with a strong hand, and with an outstretched arm;

for his loving kindness endures forever:

to him who divided the Red Sea apart;

for his loving kindness endures forever;

and made Israel to pass through the middle of it;

for his loving kindness endures forever;

but overthrew Pharaoh and his army in the Red Sea; for his loving kindness endures forever:

to him who led his people through the wilderness;

for his loving kindness endures forever:
to him who struck great kings;
for his loving kindness endures forever;
and killed mighty kings;
for his loving kindness endures forever:
Sihon king of the Amorites;
for his loving kindness endures forever;
Og king of Bashan;
for his loving kindness endures forever;
and gave their land as an inheritance;
for his loving kindness endures forever;
even a heritage to Israel his servant;
for his loving kindness endures forever:
who remembered us in our low estate;
for his loving kindness endures forever;
and has delivered us from our adversaries;
for his loving kindness endures forever:
who gives food to every creature;
for his loving kindness endures forever.
Oh give thanks to the God of heaven;
for his loving kindness endures forever.

Part 2

Seulchen Orech – The Meal
The Egg

We begin the meal with the roasted egg dipped in saltwater to show the new life offered to the Israelites in the Promised Land; a new life born out of many tears and heartaches. Added to the Passover celebration during the exile in Babylon, the egg stands as a reminder of the obstacles and hardships in Jewish history and Adonai's provision.

We eat this meal in royal fashion to demonstrate that we are no longer slaves, but a free people, the royal people. For in fact, all who believe have become children of God. John 1:12-13 (NIV) acknowledges, "To all who received Him, to those who believed in His Name, He gave the right to become children of God – children born not of natural descent, nor of human decisions, or a husband's will, but born of God."

Celebrant: Eat the meal starting with the roasted egg. Next, Matzo ball soup ... after the meal is finished, complete the Haggadah.

After the meal is finished, continue with the Haggadah.

חי

Tzaphun – The Afikomen

Earlier in the service, the middle piece of matzo was broken and hidden. At this time, the children need to find the afikomen so that it can become the conclusion of the Passover dinner. After this, nothing may be eaten until breakfast tomorrow. Traditionally, the child who finds the afikomen bargains with the Celebrant for a prize before the child returns the afikomen. Therefore, I ask the children (twelve and under) who would like to look for the afikomen to do so.

Celebrant: Pause to allow for the children to scurry about looking for the hidden afikomen. When one child brings the afikomen back, then a prize is given to that child.

Each of us must eat a small piece of the afikomen demonstrating that each one of us must personally be involved with Adonai's redemption. We remember that if Adonai had not delivered the Israelites out of Egypt, then many of us would be slaves today. Likewise, without Yeshua's death, we would be slaves to our sins today.

The afikomen has a three-fold significance. First, this piece of matzo represents the Messiah, Yeshua, separated from the group, broken, and hidden. Yeshua taught in John 6:48-51 (WEB) that, "I am the bread of life. Your fathers ate the manna in the wilderness, and they died. This is the bread which comes down out of heaven, that anyone may eat of it and not die. I am the living bread which came down out of heaven. If anyone eats of this bread, he will live forever."

Celebrant: Break the afikomen into small bite size pieces. Place one per person onto a plate and pass the plate around the table. Everyone should take a piece of the afikomen. We will postpone eating the matzo for a few moments.

Second, just as the word afikomen means to come after, likewise, Yeshua's resurrection came after three days in the tomb. Yeshua explained, "It is written, that the Christ [the Messiah, the Anointed] would suffer and rise from the dead on the third day" (Luke 24:46, AMP). Therefore, it remains appropriate for a child to find the afikomen after the meal. Furthermore, just as a child finds the afikomen and receives a prize, so we must come to Yeshua as a little child. Anyone finding the Messiah, Yeshua, finds a true treasure. Anyone finding Yeshua finds eternal life! Ironically, Yeshua still remains hidden from the eyes of many people. As Paul points out in Romans 11:7-8 (WEB), "God gave them a spirit of stupor, eyes that they should not see, and ears that they should not hear, to this very day." These people have not yet received the afikomen.

Third, because the afikomen is the last thing eaten, we understand that the work of Yeshua on the cross remains the last thing necessary to ensure our salvation. Nothing else can be added to the work of Yeshua; nothing can replace the work of Yeshua. "For God so loved the world that He gave His only and unique Son, so that everyone who trusts in Him may have eternal life, instead of being utterly destroyed. For God did not send the Son into the world to judge the world, but rather so that through Him, the world might be saved" (John 3:16-17, CJB).

After the meal almost two thousand years ago, the last piece of matzo was distributed to those around the table. Then Yeshua said, "This is my body which is given for you. Do this in memory of me" (Luke 22:19, WEB).

Celebrant: Hold up the matzo.

Blessed are You Lord God, King of the Universe, who bring for the bread from the earth. Amen.

Baruch atah, Adonai Eloheinu, Melech haolam, hamotzee lechem min haaretz. Amen.

ברוך אתה אדוני, אלוהים מלך העולם, המוציא לחם מן הארץ.

Let us now eat the afikomen for this is the first part of Yeshua's communion.

Optional Song: We Will Glorify by Twila Paris (1982)

We will glorify the King of kings

We will glorify the Lamb

We will glorify the Lord of lords

Who is the great I am

Lord Jehovah reigns in majesty

We will bow before His throne

We will worship Him in righteousness

We will worship Him alone

The Third Cup – The Cup of Redemption

After the afikomen comes the third cup, the Cup of Redemption or the Cup of the Passover Lamb. Traditionally, the Cup of Redemption commemorates the splitting of the sea after Moses stretched out his arms and the Israelites crossed the sea on dry land. Subsequently, the Israelites received freedom and complete redemption from slavery.

During a Passover, Yeshua lifted the third cup, the cup of the Passover lamb, the Cup of Redemption, and said, "Drink from it, all of you. This is my blood of the covenant, which is poured out for many for the forgiveness of sins" (Matthew 26:27-28, NIV). As Moses stretched his arms to save the Israelites, so Yeshua's arms would be outstretched to bring salvation to His people. Just as it was critical that the Passover lamb's blood be on the lintel and doorposts in the sign of a cross while the Hebrew's waited to be released from their bondage in Egypt, so also, it was critical that the perfect sacrifice, the perfect Passover Lamb, shed His blood on a cross for our redemption. Leviticus 17:11 (NIV) attests, "For the life of a creature is in the blood, and I have given it to you to make atonement for yourselves on the alter; it is the blood that makes atonement for one's life." This is Yeshua's communion, the cup of Redemption, the promise started in Genesis with the sin of Eve and ending with Yeshua's blood on the cross.

In John 6:53-57 (AMP), Yeshua said to them, "I assure you and most solemnly say to you, unless you eat the flesh of the Son of Man and drink His blood [unless you believe in Me as Savior and believe in the saving power of My blood which will be shed for you], you do not have life in yourselves. The one who eats My flesh and drinks My blood [believes in Me, accepts Me as Savior] has eternal life [that is, now possesses it], and I will raise him up [from the dead] on the last day. For My flesh is true [spiritual] food, and My blood is true [spiritual] drink. He who eats My flesh and drinks My blood [believes in Me, accepts Me as Savior] remains in Me, and I [in the same way remain] in him. Just as the living Father sent Me, and I live because of the Father, even so the one who feeds on Me [believes in Me, accepts Me as Savior] will also live because of Me."

Celebrant: Hold up the Cup of Redemption.

Let us pray, Adonai, King of the universe, we praise and bless Your name that You bring forth the fruit of the vine. We thank you that You, Adonai, have not only redeemed us from slavery, but also redeemed us from slavery to sin. We thank You for the promise of bringing us safely to the new Jerusalem. We thank You for the body and blood of the Passover lamb. Amen.

Baruch atah, Adonai Eloheinu, Melech haolam, asher bara et pri hagefen. Anu modim lecha, Adonai, ki atah lo rak gaalta otanu min avdutanu ela gam min haavdot lachet. Anu modim lecha al hahvtachah leyerushalaem chadasha. Anu modim lecha al haguph vehadam shel tzan hapesach. Amen.

ברוך אתה אדוני אלוהינו , מלך העולם, אשר ברא את פרי הגפן. אנו מודים לך, אדוני, כי אתה לא רק גאלת אותנו מן עבדותנו אלא גם מן העבדות לחטא.

אנו מודים לך על ההבטחה לירושלים חדשה. אנו מודים לך על הגוף והדם של צאן הפסח. אמן,

Let us now drink the wine for this is the second part of Yeshua's communion.

Part 3

Hillel – Grace after the Meal

Grace comes after the meal. Deuteronomy 8:10 (WEB) says, "You shall eat and be full, and you shall bless Adonai your God for the good land He has given you." In a Jewish home, the grace after the meal involves a lengthy sequence of scripture prayer.

Optional song: Psalm 113 (WEB) and 114 (WEB)

> *Praise Yah!*
> *Praise, you servants of Adonai,*
> *praise Adonai's name.*
> *Blessed be Adonai's name,*
> *from this time forward and forever more.*
> *From the rising of the sun to its going down,*
> *Adonai's name is to be praised.*
> *Adonai is high above all nations,*
> *his glory above the heavens.*
> *Who is like Adonai, our God,*
> *who has his seat on high,*
> *Who stoops down to see in heaven and in the earth?*

He raises up the poor out of the dust.

Lifts up the needy from the ash heap,

that he may set him with princes,

even with the princes of his people.

He settles the barren woman in her home

as a joyful mother of children.

Praise Yah!

When Israel went out of Egypt,

the house of Jacob from a people of foreign language,

Judah became his sanctuary,

Israel his dominion.

The sea saw it, and fled.

The Jordan was driven back.

The mountains skipped like rams,

the little hills like lambs.

What was it, you sea, that you fled?

You Jordan, that you turned back?

You mountains, that you skipped like rams;

you little hills, like lambs?

Tremble, you earth, at the presence of the Lord,

at the presence of the God of Jacob,

who turned the rock into a pool of water,

the flint into a spring of waters.

Additional optional song: Psalm 115, 116, 117, and 118 or

Adir Hu (author unknown)

> *Mighty is He! Mighty is He!*
>
> *May He build His Temple soon.*
>
> *Speedily, speedily,*
>
> *In our lifetime may it be.*
>
> *Build, o Lord! Build, O Lord!*
>
> *Build your Temple speedily!*

The Cup of Elijah

Elijah was a forerunner of the Messiah, Malachi 4:5 (WEB) prophesizes, "I will send you Elijah the prophet before the great and terrible day of" Adonai. This passage refers to the coming of Elijah prior to the eminent coming of the Messiah. Thus, the cup for Elijah holds a special place at every Passover. Throughout the Seder resides the hope that, this year, the Messiah will come. When Messiah arrives, He will save His people and fulfill the prophesy to bring all believers to Israel as promised in Deuteronomy 34:4, Psalm 107:2-3, and reconfirmed in Luke 13:29.

I ask the oldest child to open the door. During this time, the other children need to watch the cup of Elijah very carefully to see if Elijah has come. If the liquid goes down that means the Messiah is, even now, on His way. To the Jews and Christians believers, the hope is that the Messiah will come this very night.

Optional song: Days of Elijah by Robin Mark (1997)

> *These are the days of Elijah,*
>
> *Declaring the word of the Lord*
>
> *And these are the days of Your servant Moses,*
>
> *Righteousness being restored.*
>
> *And though these are days of great trial,*
>
> *Of famine and darkness and sword,*
>
> *Still, we are the voice in the desert crying*
>
> *"Prepare ye the way of the Lord!"*

The Fourth Cup: The Cup of Acceptance

As our Seder ends, we take our fourth cup of wine. The fourth cup recalls our covenant with Adonai to the tasks that still awaits us as a people called to serve. Exodus 6:7 (AMP) declares, "I will take you as My people ... I am the LORD your God, who redeemed you and brought you out from under the burdens of the Egyptians." Traditionally, the Cup of Acceptance represents the calling of Israel to become a nation, "You shall be to Me a kingdom of priests and a holy nation" (Exodus 19:5-7, WEB) at Mount Sinai.

As believers in the Lordship of Yeshua, we understand that the Cup of Acceptance centers on accepting Yeshua and becoming a child of Adonai. To anyone who believes in the Lordship of Yeshua, we as believers have been granted the right to become children of Adonai (1 John 1:11-13). The Gospel of John records Yeshua's acceptance of the fourth cup. Yeshua knowing that He fulfilled His purpose and Scripture said, "I am thirsty" (John 19:28, WEB). A jar full of cheap, sour wine stood there, so a Roman soldier soaked a sponge in the wine, coated it with oregano leaves and held it up to Yeshua's mouth. After Yeshua took the wine, Yeshua said, "It is accomplished!" (John 19:30, NIV) Then, Yeshua bowed his head and died. Thus, the Cup of Acceptance is complete.

Celebrant: All drink the fourth cup of wine.

Blessed are You oh LORD, Adonai, King of the Universe. We bless and praise Your Name for You called us to be the fruit of the vine; Your people called to serve You.

Baruch atah, Adonai Eloheinu, Melech haolam, asher bara et pri hagefen. Anu mevrecim vameshabchim et shemcha ki atah tziveta alenu lihiot pri hagefen.

ברוך אתה אדוני אלוהינו , מלך העולם, אשר ברא את פרי הגפן. אנו מברכים ומשבחים את שמך כי אתה ציוות עלינו להיות פרי הגפן.

חי

Conclusion

The Seder service has come and gone; its rights observed in full. We wait another year for the redemption of Israel. For centuries, the heart cry from the Jews proclaimed, 'Next year in Jerusalem!' But something shifted, a cry sounds from all continents, a groan from the hearts of His people, 'This year in Jerusalem! This year, come Messiah come!' As believers we also look forward to the day when we can celebrate our redemption. In the same manner, 'Come Yeshua!' exists as a cry from the heart of every believer.

Blessed are you, O LORD, our God, King of the Universe, for the vine and the fruits of the vine, for the increase of the field, and for the land which You gave our ancestors as an inheritance. Have compassion on us, O LORD, our God. Have compassion on Your people, on Jerusalem, on Zion, on the tabernacle of Your Glory, on Your alter, and on Your temple. O LORD, our God, bless us in holiness and purity and cause us to rejoice on this day of the Feast of Unleavened Bread. For You, O LORD,

are good and beneficent to all. Therefore, we thank you for the land and the fruit of the vine.

Baruch atah, Adonai Eloheinu, Melech haolam, al hagefen vepri hagefen, al gidol hasaday veal Haaretz shahorashta laavotinu khirosha. Terachem alinu Elohinu, terachem al enashaka, al yarushalim, tsion, al mishkan tahilatka, al mizbachka veal beit miqodeshka. Elohim, beracanu baqodesh vatohar vatigrom lanu lismoach bayom haza shel tsom hamatsot. Mishum shaatah, Elohim, tov vemoail lekol. Leken anu modim lakha al haadamah veal peri hagefen.

ברוך אתה אדוני, אלוהינו מלך העולם, על הגפן ופרי הגפן, על גידול השדה ועל הארץ שהורשת לאבותינו כירושה.

תרחם עלינו אלוהינו, תרחם על אנשיך, על ירושלים, ציון, על משכן תהילתך , על מזבחך ועל בית מקדשך. אלוהים, ברכנו בקודש וטוהר ותגרום לנו לשמוח ביום הזה של צום המצות. משום שאתה, אלוהים, טוב ומועיל לכל. לכן אנו מודים לך על האדמה ועל פרי הגפן.

"May Adonai bless you and keep you. May Adonai make His face shine on you and show you His Favor. May Adonai lift up His face toward you and grant you His peace."

(Numbers 6:24-26 – the Aaronic Blessing)

Yevarchecha Adonai veyismarcha. Yaer Adonai panav alecha vaichanecha. Yisa Adonai, panav elecha vayashim lecha shalom.

יברכך יהוה וישמרך. יאר יהוה פניו אליך ויחנך.
ישא יהוה פניו אליך וישם לך שלום.

To Adonai be the glory, the honor and the dominion both now and forever! Amen.

Appendix

Appendix I: The Questions

Child 1: Why is this night different from all other nights? On all other nights we eat either leavened bread or unleavened bread; on this night, why do we eat only unleavened bread?

Child 2: On all other nights, we eat all kinds of herbs; why on this night do we eat bitter herbs?

Child 3: On all other nights, we do not dip our herbs at all; why on this night do we dip them?

Child 4: On all other nights, we eat in an ordinary manner; why tonight, do we dine with special ceremony?

Appendix II: Glossary

Adonai – The Jewish title of reverence for the God of Abraham, Isaac, and Jacob.

Gentiles – A person who is not Jewish.

Haggadah – The liturgy for the Seder service held during the Jewish Festival of Unleavened Bread commonly referred to as the Passover.

Jewish Calendar – A calendar based on a lunar year and used dominantly for Jewish religious observances. In Israel, it provides an agricultural time frame for planting and harvest.

Leavened – Typically thought of as a substance that causes fermentation or expansion of dough but can include an element (sin) that produces and altering influence.

Passover – also known as *Pesach*. Passover is a Jewish festival that commemorates the flight of the Israelites from Egypt during the time of Moses. The festival includes the eating of unleavened bread. Passover begins on the 14th day of Nisan in the Jewish calendar and often coincides with 'holy week' in the Christian calendar.

Pesach – The Jewish word for Passover.

Polytheistic – a religious doctrine that maintains that many gods exist.

Seder – the ceremonial dinner that commemorates the flight of the Israelites from Egypt in the times of Moses. It includes reading the liturgical Haggadah and eating symbolic foods. Seder is commonly held on the first night of the Passover festival.

Yeshua – the Hebrew name for Jesus of Nazareth.

Yahweh – the actual name of Adonai. In the Jewish tradition, the actual name of God is considered sacred and holy. Therefore, the name 'Adonai' is substituted throughout the text the term for the name Yahweh. *"Yud-Heh-Vav-Heh [ADONAI] ... This is My name forever"* (Exodus 3:15, CJB).

חי - the Hebrew word means 'life'. John 5:24 (WEB) explains, "He who hears My word and believes Him who sent Me has eternal life, and doesn't come into judged, but has passed out of death into life."

Appendix III: Song Lyrics

Optional songs exist throughout the Haggadah. I included both traditional songs and some 'newer' ones that seem appropriate within the Seder.

Adir Hu (author unknown)

Note: Adir Hu is a traditional song, dating back to 15th century Germany, about the restoration of Zion and building the Temple. Ironically, while the Jewish people traditionally think of building the Temple as referring to the Temple in Jerusalem, as a Messianic believer, the desire for Adonai to build the temple is to introspectively evaluate how we evangelize or disciple the people around us. What am I doing to help build the Kingdom of God?

(Optional song after the Hillel – Grace after the Meal)

Mighty is He! Mighty is He!

May He build His Temple soon.

Speedily, speedily,

In our lifetime may it be.

Build, o Lord! Build, O Lord!

Build your Temple speedily!

Chosen, great, renowned is He!
May He build His Temple soon.
Speedily, speedily.
In our lifetime may it be.
Build, o Lord! Build, O Lord!
Build your Temple speedily!

Glorious, faithful, pure is He!
May He build His Temple soon.
Speedily, speedily,
In our lifetime may it be.
Build, o Lord! Build, O Lord!
Build your Temple speedily!

Righteous, faultless, One is He!
May He build His Temple soon.
Speedily, speedily,
In our lifetime may it be.
Build, o Lord! Build, O Lord!
Build your Temple speedily!

Humble in kingship,

Redeeming as of right;

To Him the righteous sing:

"To you, just to you,

To you and to you alone;

To you, yes, only to you,

To you, O LORD, is sovereignty."

To God praise belongs;

To Him it is ever due.

Holy is kingship,

Merciful as of right'

To Him His myriad hosts sing:

"To you, just to you,

To you and to you alone;

To you, yes, only to you,

To you, O LORD, is sovereignty."

To God praise belongs;

To Him it is ever due.

All-powerful in kingship,

Sustaining as of right;

To Him the upright sing:

"To you, just to you,

To you and to you alone;

To you, yes, only to you,

To you, O LORD, is sovereignty."

To God praise belongs;

To Him it is ever due.

All -pure in kingship, Powerful as of tight;

To Him His courtiers sing:

"To you, just to you,

To you and to you alone;

To you, yes, only to you,

To you, O LORD, is sovereignty."

To God praise belongs;

To Him it is ever due.

One alone in kingship,

Mighty as of right;

To Him His disciples sing:

"To you, just to you,

To you and to you alone;

To you, yes, only to you,

To you, O LORD, is sovereignty."

To God praise belongs;

To Him it is ever due.

Exalted in Kingship,

Revered as on right;

To Him His angels sing:

"To you, just to you,

To you and to you alone;

To you, yes, only to you,

To you, O LORD, is sovereignty."

To God praise belongs;

To Him it is ever due.

Public Domain. Retrieved from
http://www.happypassover.net/passover-music/adir-hu.html

And It Came to Pass at Midnight (Author Unknown)

This song's first written record appears in an 11th century Italian Haggadah as a poem. Numerous versions for this song exist.

(*Optional song after the 10 plagues*)

In the days of old you performed many miracles at night.

In the early watch of evening, on this night.

To gain the victory, Abraham divided his army at night. (Genesis 14:15)

And it came to pass at midnight.

You judged Abimelech, king of Gerar, in a dream during the night; (Genesis 20:3)

You struck Laban, the Syrian, with terror in the night; (Genesis 20:3)

Israel wrestled with an angel and prevailed at night. (Genesis 32:25)

And it came to pass at midnight.

Egypt's first-born you smote at night; (Exodus 12:29)

The Egyptians found themselves powerless when they arose at night.

You scattered Sisera's army, aided by the stars of night. (Judges 5:20)

It came to pass a midnight.

Sennacherib's army was decimated at night.
(II Kings 19:35)
Babylon's god, Bel and his pillar crashed in the night,
(Isaiah 46:1-2)

Mysteries were revealed to Daniel in a vision at night.
(Daniel 2:19)

It came to pass at midnight.

Drunken Belshazzar was slain at night; (Daniel 5:30)
Daniel, saved from the lions' dem, interpreted the dreams of night. (Daniel 6:24)

Hateful Haman wrote his edicts at night. (Ester 3:12)

It came to pass at midnight.

You triumphed over Haman when sleep failed Ahasuerus at night. (Ester 6:1)

You tread down the enemy for him who asked:

"Watchman, what of the night?" (Isaiah 63:3, 21:11)

You will like the watchman; The morning comes as well as the night." (Isaiah 21:12)

It came to pass at midnight.

Hasten the day which is neither day nor night;

(Zechariah 14:7)

Most High, proclaim that you are the day, and you are also the night.

Place watchmen to guard the city, day and night.

(Isaiah 62:6)

Make bright as day the darkness of the night.

May it come to pass at midnight.

Sevener, H.A. (Eds.). (n.d.). *Messianic Passover Haggadah*. New York, NY: Chosen People Ministries.

Awesome God by Rich Mullins

(Optional song for after the first cup – the Cup of Sanctification)

(Chorus only)

Our God is an awesome God

He reigns from heaven above

With wisdom, power, and love

Our God is an awesome God

Our God is an awesome God

He reigns from heaven above

With wisdom, power, and love

Our God is an awesome God

Mullins, R. Lyrics to "Awesome God." *Winds of Heaven, Stuff of Earth*, 1988. Retrieved from https://genius.com/4900508

Dayenu (Author Unknown)

Note: Originating in the 9th century, Dayenu remains an extremely popular Passover song. It tells of the great, miraculous things that Adonai did for the Israelites. Yet, I ask ... would a singular miracle really suffice? History confirms that 'it was never enough' not a singular miracle and not the summation of the miracles. Repeatedly, the Jewish people turned away from Adonai ... only the remnant remained.

(Optional song for after the four questions)

If He had brought us out from Egypt,

and had not carried out judgments against them - It would have sufficed!

If He had carried out judgments against them,

and not against their idols - It would have sufficed!

If He had destroyed their idols,

and had not smitten their first-born   It would have sufficed!

If He had smitten their first-born,

and had not given us their wealth - It would have sufficed!

Dayenu, it would have sufficed!

If He had given us their wealth,

and had not split the sea for us - It would have sufficed!

If He had split the sea for us,

and had not taken us through it on dry land - It would have sufficed!

If He had taken us through the sea on dry land,

and had not drowned our oppressors in it - It would have sufficed!

If He had drowned our oppressors in it,

and had not supplied our needs in the desert for forty years - It would have sufficed!

Dayenu, it would have sufficed!

If He had supplied our needs in the desert for forty years,

and had not fed us the manna - It would have sufficed!

If He had fed us the manna,

and had not given us the Shabbat - It would have sufficed!

If He had given us the Shabbat,

and had not brought us before Mount Sinai - It would have sufficed!

If He had brought us before Mount Sinai,

and had not given us the Torah - It would have sufficed!

Dayenu, it would have sufficed!

If He had given us the Torah,

and had not brought us into the land of Israel - It would have sufficed!

If He had brought us into the land of Israel,

and not built for us the Holy Temple – It would have sufficed!

Dayenu, it would have sufficed!

Public Domain. Retrieved from
https://www.aish.com/h/pes/t/si/48937752.html

Days of Elijah by Robin Mark (1997)

(Optional song for after the Cup of Elijah)

These are the days of Elijah,

Declaring the word of the Lord

And these are the days of Your servant Moses,

Righteousness being restored.

And though these are days of great trial,

Of famine and darkness and sword,

Still, we are the voice in the desert crying

"Prepare ye the way of the Lord!"

Behold He comes riding on the clouds,

Shining like the sun at the trumpet call,

Lift your voice, it's the year of jubilee,

And out of Zion's hill salvation comes.

These are the days of Ezekiel,

The dry bones becoming as flesh,

And these are the days of Your servant David,

Rebuilding a temple of praise.

These are the days of the harvest,

The fields are as white in Your world,

And we are the laborers in Your vineyard,

Declaring the word of the Lord!

Mark, R (1997) Lyrics to "Days of Elijah." *Room for Grace [Live]*, 1997. Retrieved from https://robinmark.com/days-of-elijah/

O Come, O Come Emmanuel by JM Neale (1861)

(Optional song for after breaking the middle piece of matzo)

O come, o come, Emmanuel,

And ransom captive Israel,

That mourns in lonely exile here

Until the Son of God appear.

Rejoice! Rejoice! Emmanuel

Shall come to thee, O Israel.

O come, Thou Rod of Jesse, free

Thine own from Satan's tyranny;

From depths of hell your people save,

And give them victory over the grave.

Rejoice! Rejoice! Emmanuel

Shall come to thee, O Israel.

O come, Thou Day Spring, come and cheer

Our spirits by Thine advent here;

Disperse the gloomy clouds of night

And death's dark shadows put to flight!

Rejoice! Rejoice! Emmanuel

Shall come to thee, O Israel.

O come, Thou Key of David, come,

And open wide our heavenly home;

Make safe the way that leads on high,

And close the path to misery.

Rejoice! Rejoice! Emmanuel

Shall come to thee, O Israel.

O come, o come, Thou Lord of Might,

Who to Thy tribes on Sinai's height;

In ancient times didst give the law

In cloud, and majesty, and awe.

Rejoice! Rejoice! Emmanuel

Shall come to thee, O Israel.

Neale, JM (1861, translated). O Come, O Come Emmanuel. Retrieved from https://genius.com/Christmas-songs-o-come-o-come-emmanuel-lyrics

We will Glorify the King of Kings by Twila Paris (1982)

(Optional song for after eating the afikomen)

We will glorify the King of kings

We will glorify the Lamb

We will glorify the Lord of lords

Who is the great I am

Lord Jehovah reigns in majesty

We will bow before His throne

We will worship Him in righteousness

We will worship Him alone

We will glorify the King of kings

We will glorify the Lamb

We will glorify the Lord of lords

Who is the great I am

He is Lord of Heaven, Lord of Earth

He is Lord of all who live

He is Lord above the universe

All praise to Him we give

Oh, hallelujah…

Paris, T. Lyrics to "We Will Glorify the King of Kings." *Keepin' My Eyes on You*, 1982. Retrieved from https://www.lyricsfreak.com/t/twila+paris/we+will+glorify_20349942.html

Appendix IV: Instructions

For the Celebrant:

Traditionally, the Passover Seder remains a home-bound celebration. Yet, the meal and Haggadah can adapt to accommodate larger groups. The Celebrant can assume the liberty of assigning or distributing different sections (i.e. the ten plagues) of the Haggadah to various people. The Seder segments into three sections: the Passover story and the Seder plate, the meal, and the Cups of Redemption and Acceptance. In total, we plan about three hours for the Passover Seder.

For the cook and individuals that prepares for the Seder:

First, do not stress. This is a feast for the LORD. It belongs to God. Relax and know that He is God, not the meal. It is a time of fun, laughter, freedom, and liberty. The first segment of Passover takes about one to 1 ½ hours so prepare the food to accommodate the delay in serving. Crockpots, roasters, ovens on low temperature, and simmer continue to be great options for keeping the food warm. For cold foods, use the refrigerator, opt for the garage, or outdoor porch (if you are in a cold climate area during this season). If constricted finances render a formal dinner not an option, move to a more casual meal. While a bowl of soup and crackers might be considered sacrilegious by some people, the purpose behind the Passover is to remember the power of Adonai and what He did. Do not fret over what you do not have. Gift Adonai with a heart of thanksgiving for who Adonai is and what Adonai did! We received great gifts: the gift of freedom, the gift of Yeshua, the gift of freedom for our souls.

The tables requirements (preferred):

In the home, a formal table setting remains dominant. Many families reserve formal china and silverware for Passover only; some families use their best place settings in a formal style. Because we are commanded to "train up a child in the way he should go" (Proverb 22:6, WEB), we enjoyed teaching our children about formal dining within the Passover setting. A formal place setting includes: 2 plates, 2 spoons, one knife, 2 forks, an additional fork or spoon dependent upon the dessert, one soup bowl, one water glass, one wine goblet, and a folded napkin. Our children loved the formal setting and enjoyed experimenting with different fancy napkin folds. Consequently, when our children encountered multiple silverware and formal dining events as college students and in their careers, they were prepared for the challenge.

- Tablecloth - traditionally white
- Wine (grape juice) - each person to drink four cups
- Place settings – include soup bowl, 2 food plates (one for the ceremonial food and one for the meal

stacked on top of each other), forks, spoons, knife, 2 glasses: one for water and one for wine
- Matzo, three whole matzo pieces that are wrapped. (Set the wrapped matzo immediately to the right of the Seder plate.) The three matzos wrap are in a unique fashion: Use a long, white linen cloth, tea towel length. Place the first matzo on the short edge of the cloth, fold the cloth over the matzo (one time). Place the next matzo on top of the other matzo with the cloth between them. reverse fold the linen cloth over the 2nd matzo. Place the 3rd matzo on top of the other two matzo. Then, cover with the linen cloth. In appearance the cloth zigzags between the matzo. Then gently fold the linen cloth over the sides of the matzo and place on a plate by the Celebrant's place setting. For use throughout the meal in various sections
- An Elijah's cup filled with wine (grape juice) to be used in the Cup of Elijah section
- A set of white candles in holders and matches (set in front of the place setting for the individual assigned to light the candles). For use in the Lighting of Candles – *Brechat Haner*

- A prize for the child that finds the hidden afikomen (i.e. gift cards, candy, bike, your choice)
- A pitcher of water, a basin to catch the water, and a towel to dry hands (to be used in the Washing of the Hands section)

The Seder Plate:

The plate pictured above was purchased in Israel as a gift from our son. Seder plates can be purchased online, but we used a normal dinner plate upon which sat small glass bowls to hold the Seder items prior to being gifted our Seder plate. The items on the Seder plate include:

- Salty water - one small bowl to dip the parsley, use enough salt that it tastes like tears
- Fresh parsley – a sprig for each person

- Shank bone – one for the Seder plate (our daughter 3D printed the one we use)
- Egg - one egg per person (traditionally roasted, but hard boiled will work)
- Horseradish – enough so that each person can eat some two times during the Seder meal
- Charoseth – enough so that each person can eat some one time with the Seder plate and additional charoseth for during the Seder meal

The Passover Seder Menu:

The Passover Seder is NOT a typical pot-luck meal. Honoring kosher requirements during the Seder Meal serves to elevate the importance and significance of the meal since many of the foods tend to be "unusual" in our normal diets. Therefore, making the meal special. Please note that the Passover Seder is segmented into three units with the meal being the center unit. Usually, the first segment extends about one to 1 ½ hours during which the ceremonial foods are eaten.

Do not prepare anything that contains:

- Pig (pork, ham, sausage, lard)

- Shellfish (shrimp, oysters, crab, or any other items with shellfish as an ingredients)
- Yeast (bread, rolls, bagels, pretzels, some crackers, pasta, noodles, chips, croutons, breadcrumbs, processed soups, or anything with yeast or leavening as an ingredient)
- Dairy products (milk, butter, creams)

Passover recipes are available on from number of online resources: Suggestions include:

- Matzo ball soup
- Meat: Roasted lamb or Chicken
- New potatoes with parsley
- Honey glazed carrots
- Green lettuce salad – with a non-diary product dressing
- Fresh fruit or fruit salad
- Vegetables or vegetable salad
- Charoseth (needed for the Seder plate, but make enough for everyone to enjoy with the meal)
- Desert of date squares or toffee bars
  Drinks:
- Do NOT use the wine (grape juice) with the meal

- Water is preferred - prefill the glasses and set water pitchers on the tables
- Coffee or tea (optional), but no dairy is allowed

Acknowledgements

Wow! Abba Father, You are great! Nothing could adequately express what You have done. I pray that succeeding generations see with eyes, void of scales, the glorious events You have and will perform. Adonai declares in Isaiah 59:21 (WEB), "this is My covenant with them ... My Spirit who is on you, and My words which I put in your mouth shall not depart from your mouth, nor out of the mouth of your offspring, nor out of the mouth of your offspring's offspring."

To Jim, my husband, thank you for your patience and all the dinners you cooked while I wrote, researched, and rewrote. You, Jim, are one of the greatest gifts God gave me. Gabe, Mike, Rose, Nate, and Zack, thank you for your encouragement, demands that everything be written down, and constant suggestions. This Haggadah exists because you saw the vision!

To my editors: Carol, Elvina, Gabe, Gina, Jim, Nate, Rose, Sue and Zack. Thank you for keeping me on task. To Nate, my resident (although living in Jerusalem) biblical scholar and son, your ability to translate and verify

Hebrew script was a significant blessing. To Rose, our daughter, 'fun' analysist, and the individual whom 3D printed the shank bone for our home Passover celebration, thank you for your encouragement, friendship, and ability to have fun. To Zack, our son, thank you for teaching me the importance of keeping the festival. Finally, my heart felt gratitude to our family's catalyst, Joel and Linda, who taught our family that our GREAT GOD exists!

Chris enjoys hearing how this text impacts your life or perceptions. You can reach her at chris.steinmeyerind@gmail.com or through her blog at www.beyondabrace.wordpress.com.

Made in the USA
Middletown, DE
23 March 2023